CW00549424

STILL LIFE WITH FEEDING SNAKE

STILL LIFE WITH
FEEDING SNAKE

John Burnside

CAPE POETRY

1 3 5 7 9 10 8 6 4 2

Jonathan Cape, an imprint of Vintage Publishing,
20 Vauxhall Bridge Road,
London SW1V 2SA

Jonathan Cape is part of the Penguin Random House
group of companies whose addresses can be found at
global.penguinrandomhouse.com

First published by Jonathan Cape in 2017

www.vintage-books.co.uk

A CIP catalogue record for this book is available
from the British Library

ISBN 9781910702413

Typeset in India by Thomson Digital Pvt Ltd, Noida, Delhi

Printed and bound in Great Britain by TJ International Ltd, Padstow, Cornwall

Penguin Random House is committed to a sustainable future for
our business, our readers and our planet. This book is made
from Forest Stewardship Council® certified paper.

For Michael Krüger

Si rectum cor tuum esset, tunc omnis creatura speculum vitæ et liber sanctæ doctrinæ esset.

Thomas à Kempis

What we do see depends mainly on what we look for.

John Lubbock

CONTENTS

STILL LIFE WITH FEEDING SNAKE

THE BEAUTIES OF NATURE
AND THE WONDERS OF THE
WORLD WE LIVE IN

And Ananias went his way, and entered into the house; and putting his hands on him said, Brother Saul, the Lord, even Jesus, that appeared unto thee in the way as thou camest, hath sent me, that thou mightest receive thy sight, and be filled with the Holy Ghost.

Acts of the Apostles

I'm haunted by the story of a man
who, blind since birth,
was gifted with new sight, his surgeon
pointing out the things he'd only known
by name till then: the roses in a vase,
a window filled with light,
his daughter's eyes.
One story says
it wasn't what he'd hoped,
and later, in the house he'd thought so clean
and spacious – dirty now, and cramped –
the birds he used to feed seemed dull
and vulnerable to cats, the photograph
they told him was a portrait of his wife
so ugly, and unlike the voice he'd heard
for years, it seemed
the cruellest of deceits.
Sometimes, they would find him in a makeshift
blindfold, just to have the darkness back,
the world in scent and touch
and measured steps, a theatre of black
to match the black he loved
inside his head.

On moonless nights, he climbed up to the loft
and gazed into the sky above his house,
well-deep and still
and innocent of stars.

When Saul fell from his horse,
it would have seemed
a mishap, nothing more,
to those he rode with.
Some of his companions would have laughed,
then waited
till he got back on his feet
to crack a joke,
but when at last
he rose up from the earth,
he saw no man,
and, troubled now, they led him by the hand
into Damascus.
He lay down in the darkness of himself
three days and nights, then Ananias came
to make him whole
and fill him with the spirit;
but reading of his fall
in Bible class, I liked the man he was
when he was blind,
no longer sure that mastery is all,
still unconvinced
that God would take his side.

I had my doubts
on other matters, too,
mostly the presence of God
in all our lives,
like the five crates of free school milk
in the playground at break,
or the man who came round every week

to collect the insurance.
My mother would offer him tea
and a caramel wafer,
and he would decline, every time,
with a well-tried phrase,
like *thanks all the same*, or
I'll have to be getting along.
God was like that, I thought,
though not so polite,
and it did me no good at all
when Sister Veronica
itemised all of the wonders that He had provided
everywhere, designed by His Own Hand.
No poem lovely
as a tree, she said
(though I'd never once thought to compare),
and how, in a world without God, could a boy like me
explain the complex beauty
of the eye?

When Saul was taken out
for execution,
he borrowed a shawl
from someone in the crowd
and covered his face, to have
one moment by himself
before the sword.
Did he whisper goodbye
to the earth, to its scents and winds,
or did he think forward to heaven
and wonder how much difference there is
between the play of sunlight in a stand
of fig-trees
and the light of the hereafter?
When death came
it cut through the flesh,

but left a perfect likeness of his face
indelibly imprinted in the shawl,
so when they held it up
the light shone through,
darkly, at first, like something seen through glass,
but later, when they leaned in,
clear as day.

Eventually, that blind man learned to see
a different world, the finer shades of rain
on stone or asphalt, market traders calling
back and forth, their lamps dimmed
one by one,
the last bus idling softly in its usual
circuit of gold and oil
on Union Road,
streamers of blue
and citrus blown through the scrawl
of blackened thorn around the drying green
where, now, the lines
are empty, office shirts
and blouses taken in
for days that pass like notes played on a scale
in music practice, fields of warmth and shade
ascending, as they must,
to aery nothing.
Somewhere along his street
an owl calls from some *Ancien Régime*
of drift and weather, texture,
masonry;
and, since it's all he has
to keep his place
in this life, which is not the gift he sought,
he loves it, all the wonder in this world
that he can bear, not
well, but well enough.

ABIDING MEMORIES OF
CHRISTIAN ZEAL

The body as the sum of all nostalgias.
Empire of footfalls; Mother as Script and Ideal

– and love no chance event, no accidental
stir of wings, or blueprint spiked with hospice.

What hymn tunes come to mind
at Candlemas, the fence wires rimmed with ice,

our plum tree medieval in the first
blue gloaming?

What carol for the kill-site, sodden plumage
scattered in the grass, and beautiful?

Always, the meadow is now: the chill after dusk,
hunter and hunted pausing in the fog

to listen, summer
barbering the skin.

Above us, souls are wandering in space;
we know them all by name: the cosmonauts,

the lonely dogs unspooling into depths
we've talked about for months, the quiet-spoken

airmen from Ohio, voices trained
to sound, on updates home, like bottled rain.

Such comfort in their dying far from earth,
entry, for those who dare, to Everafter,

its backroom of bottled tumours inch-deep in must,
its bus routes through the windy seaside towns

setting us down where death lives like a long lost
cousin, spinsterish

and hungry, though those hands we thought would burn
like ice, or venom, when they reached to touch,

are smooth and cool, not feverish at all:
Ice Queen as Rescue; Far Cry as Seventh Son.

SIRENS

History says I was born on the last day of winter,
thick snow lining the roads when my mother arrived
at Queen Margaret's, the gardens at Whitefield

empty, but for the fox she glimpsed
in passing, its lapis footprints crossing a lawn
at the edge of Dunfermline town, the new fur

tawny and fine as silk when it turned
to glance at the flashing lights, alone in the world
it was made for, a mortal dominion

where humans no longer belonged.
That was the Year of the Ram. In an old magazine
she had found in a doctor's waiting room she read

that I would be *thoughtful, creative, persevering*;
and she already had a picture of me in her mind
when they started induction:

a man walking home from work – a designer, say –
he crosses the street to buy
some blue-veined or goat's milk cheese and a bottle of Muscat,

or maybe a box of truffles, topped
with ginger and candied peel,
as a gift for his wife.

His eldest girl sings in the choir.
He picks her up after practice at nine o'clock:
white stars over the church, the night wind

tracking them home in the twilight
through seed-fall or snow.
Weekends, they go to the sea, to Capel le Ferne

or Walberswick.
He paints in oils. His wife takes photographs.
Nothing can touch this happy-ever-after.

A neighbour drove us back to Cowdenbeath, my mother
anaemic and sleepless, staring out over the fields,
all mud and puddled grass – no fox in sight,

only a flock of sheep in a farmer's yard
and the dairyman out on his rounds, with his horse and cart,
spring rain blurring the traces, the facedrop

glinting. Memory says the next ten years
was salt air and rain,
satsumas, the taste of dripping,

ball games in the tract between the prefabs,
the Gospel of Matthew, Leviticus,
Lorna Doone;

though, in truth, I remember little, and nothing for sure,
before that evening on the Old Perth Road
when someone I didn't know, a man from Lochgelly,

was thrown off his Honda Superhawk 305
and lay on the pavement dying, while somebody ran
to the one house on Blackburn Drive

that had a phone. Slowly, it seemed,
he faded, like a stain,
and I didn't know what to do, the other driver

standing away in the half-light, our home woods
empty and suddenly distant, the wind-streaked
oat fields on the far side of the verge

darkening about me where I stood,
a well-bred child, not wishing to intrude,
but hoping not to seem indifferent.

Later, I heard he was on his way back from the coast,
where his girlfriend lived, the Honda his prize
possession – *just a boy*, my mother said –

but I thought of him as a gift, his eyes dimming out
as I watched, at the quiet limit of my world,
a kinship of sorts between us, right at the end,

when the ambulance came too late
and I knew he was dead.

SELF PORTRAIT AS BLUE BABY

We came from distant space, even what some might call somewhat
of another dimension, and we are about to return from whence we
came. It requires, if you move into that evolutionary kingdom, that
you leave behind everything of human ways, human behaviour,
human ignorance, human misinformation. If I would title this
tape, it would be 'Last Chance to Evacuate Planet Earth Before
It Is Recycled'.

Marshall Applewhite

I   AUTOBIOGRAPHY

I was barely conceived in the arid
lull of the oxygen tent,
my name written out in sand, my dead
attentive, at the wet edge of the light,

but later, in the lovely
coffin of the year's last blossoming,
my body rose again
as bread and wine,

the film reel
from the shoreline of my birth
speckled with motion
and sleet-streaked, like the future.

No one can bid us love. However skilled
the skin becomes
at leaving be, there is no true
abandon.

So, all regrets aside, let's just assume
I came from distant space.
How else explain the blue? how else explain
this silken chill, like snowfall at the heart?

I wake in the dark and go from bed to bed
stitching their eyes with cataracts and scars.

They barely stir. It seems they also dream
and, sometimes, I am almost overcome

by tenderness, the instruments so light
and perfect in my hands, it feels like love.

Daytimes, I watch, and mark how kind they are.
I hear them speak, like actors in a film;

I see them laugh
and mark how kind they are.

Strange that they never foresee
the torture to come:

strange that they keep me close
and never waver.

Yet, while I think of them
as innocents, more sinned against than sinning,

I never go so far as to regret
this skill I have, this

instinct for the blade.

Trasumanar significar per verba
non si poria; però l'essemplo basti
a cui esperïenza grazia serba

Dante Alighieri

Though in the end she settled for
a bed of pinks, a few geraniums,
the thread and bloom
of bell-vines in the fence
between us and the Glancys,

my mother's secret love was for
exotic flowers, succulent
and fleshy, red
begonias, the strangeness of the colour
purple, when it puts forth veins and hair.

I knew as much, and yet, on Mother's Day
I always brought her blue Forget-me-nots
and Tradescantias so close
to indigo, you almost saw
the dead in them, the clutch of breathlessness.

It seems I recall it still,
that struggle to breathe:
the blue of the scissors, the unexpected bleed
of sap or latex
clouding in the jar,

and how I am bound to her now, or she to me,
I cannot say,
but what I have is what we had

together, all
the pretty artefacts

of sleep and superstition, fingerprints
in glassware, animal
horizons lit with frost, the cold
exemplum
in each blueprint of the heart.

I am the boy who stole the sodium
and dropped a single grain
into the fish tank.

Forgive me; but I never thought of this
as malice,

only another instance of that idiom
where anything intact is set aside
as inadmissible.

Dead in his cot, my brother only woke
much later, when his systems

failed, and he went drifting amongst stars
that no one else could see,

leaving me here, in the shell of a Russian
space suit, regulation
orange, so no matter how I try

I'll never speak that dialect again.

BLUE[1]

The day the cosmonauts fell back to earth,
radio contact gone, the bodies
dreamless in their cots, and marbled blue,

their deaths became another form
of saintliness, a charm against the flesh
the martyrs in my schoolbooks would have relished.

I must confess, I envied them a little,
alchemised souls
absorbed into starlight and cloud;

and, every night for weeks, I prayed for them,
the names on my tongue
like blisters of ash and chrism.

That year, our spindle tree cracked
and toppled in a high wind, sapwood
open to the cold, the coral berries

scattered on the lawn.
It lay there for a week until
the sun came, then I worked into the dark,

sawing it up and dragging it off to the fire,
aware, all the time,
of the house at the edge of my vision,

[1] On Jun 30, 1971, the crew of Soyuz 11 died after undocking from Salyut 1, the world's first true space station. According to official reports, the three-man crew – Georgi Dobrovolski, Viktor Patsayev and Vladislav Volkov – are the only human beings ever to die in space.

empty and still, so it seemed, though I couldn't help thinking
that someone had taken my place while I was away,
someone who might have been, had I not been,

blue as the day he was born and perfect as rain;
and the thing I most wanted, then, was to hurry inside
and find out how that presence felt

without me.
Some say true beauty is rare, and reserved for the few
– the godhead concealed in the icon, the glimpse from the
    flight-deck –

and yet it was there all along, in those fallen bodies,
in women who queued for decades in black and white
for bread rolls, or boots, or miraculous parcels of horsemeat,

and, later, in the faces of the dead
on postage stamps, that unexpected gift
for happiness that comes of being fiction.

No martyrdoms.
No holy miracles.
The true saint only asks what it is like

to fall into the world that might have been,
had it been formed
by undivided love.

They say that, before Gagarin,
there were others,
men without rank or title, boys without names

unreeling into blackness, frame by frame,
like Stations of the Cross;
but no one was there to claim them when they fell,

no generals in epaulettes and medals,
no widows and orphans, sanctioned for public grieving.
This is the heart, my mother would have said,

an empty grain store on a country road
where anything might shelter for a time
in heavy weather.

A late delivery, I sheltered for a time
in oxygen, my mother
certain that I would die, like the one before,

my predecessor, dead weight in her arms,
cradled in cotton and blue, while the midwife waited
patiently, to carry him away.

After the felling, I stripped off my working clothes
and washed at the sink, the house standing quiet behind me,
the fire at the edge of our yard

just visible, the smuts and sparks
uncanny in the stillness, wood and berries
crackling and spitting, plumes of smoke

ascending, not a breath of wind outside,
and out where the tree had been, an improbable space
at the edge of the lawn, so it seemed to me someone was there,

waiting to be released, or brought into being,
blue as the day he was born,
mon semblable; mon frère.

MEMORIES OF A NON-EXISTENT
CHILDHOOD

I could never believe in the dead,
only the blue of their houses, the fabled blue
of those who travel far into the rain
and wish for nothing,
least of all for home.

For years I was lost in the details,
heart like a flower,
tending towards the light,
the fog of the cursive,
the beauties of mistranslation.

It snowed all night between the rooms
we lived in
and the rooms we could not find.
Sometimes I laid my finger
to the chill of it, that hollow in the wall

that would not mend; sometimes I sat
for days in an upper room,
waiting for the nuthatch to appear,
the blue in the wing of it blue as the Virgin's shawl
in a painting by Tintoretto;

and, sometimes, on those winter afternoons
when everything fell still,
I sat in the chair by the door and watched
for the men in 50s raincoats, hats pulled down
and no need to show their credentials when they walked me

out to the famous road bridge, first chill of dawn,
a flight of gulls and terns crossing the bay,

and someone on the far side, just like me,
but different, his name a crude
translation of my own, his body

darker. Sooner or later, I knew,
we would be exchanged.
Code names and shadows, gestures, a foreign tongue.
Then I would cross the line and disappear,
the way I had disappeared at First Communion,

sweat on my hands and that starched white on my tongue
an incompleteness I would not refuse
for pity's sake, my mother in her shawl,
blue as the blue in a painting by Tintoretto,
mouthing the password, happy to turn me in.

Always, I am coming home
from hunting frogs or standing in the swim
of wind between the last dyke

and the sea;
         and, always, she is there,
in lanternglow,
a light that makes this world believable.

My eyes turned from the snuff
of paraffin and darkness in that house
so long ago, I barely know it's there:

washrooms wrapped in frost, a skewed moon
picking out the paths from then to now,
where someone, not myself,

goes missing, while I lie down in the warm
and wait for her to come, her hands
a labyrinth of mint and cinnamon, her book

the only book we have, the pages
thumbstained, now, with daisychain and lilac,
and such detail in the pictures, I could find

The Snow Queen, or The Lady of the Lake
so easily, it seems we must be kin.

WITH THE DISCOVERY OF COSMIC BACKGROUND RADIATION, MY BROTHER RETURNS FROM THE HEREAFTER AS A RUSSIAN COSMONAUT

You were the boy in cautionary tales
and problems in mathematics,
your voice entirely theoretical,
your face a puzzle nobody could solve.

You lived in fishponds, tyre tracks, jars of rain,
the time and tide of you a blurred
repository of what I might have been
had I been lost, or carefully unfathered.

You never understood how sweet it was
to walk out from the town at daybreak, early
summer in the woods,
a lone deer crossing your path, in its minefield of thistles.

You never kissed a girl, stayed up all night
or walked home drunk – that gold fret in your mind –
the hay market buried in snow, the town clock
ringing out the last day of the year.

Now you are floating in space,
in your orange suit,
the barest trace of carbon on your skin,
your pockets lined with chalk and apple peel.

You've been out there for years, imagining
a world you've never known:
a train stopped at the lights near Göttingen,
horses at pasture, lime pits, flights of cranes,

and all this time
I've barely pictured you,
small-boned and far in the dark,
like a sleeping bird.

Today, the birds are mostly
phantoms: collared dove and chiffchaff, sparrows
flickering in tides
across the wall,

they're nothing more than slipknots in the light
quickening into song at the edge of the garden;
and yet, it seems that something else is here,
presences implied by every shift

of wind and sunlight in this post-and-wire
that nobody looks after any more:
new animals, perhaps; or else, the thought of them,
some hint of the interspecific unpicked from the shadows.

Are these our days of heaven, in the end?
These days when the world is mostly
guessed-at, all conjecture, orphic ventures in a field
of iterance and echo, creatures

bidden from the grass to take new forms,
the absences that make us what we are
unravelled from a maze of being
heard and called for, answering and answered?

It might have been a summer's afternoon
at Crawford Hill, New Jersey, pigeons
nesting in the twenty feet of horn
antennae, built to catch the waves bounced back

from satellites; it might have been
a little later,
autumn on the way, towards the end
of 1964, a hint of frost; who knows

exactly when they started to suspect
that what they thought was local interference,
random noise, perhaps the background
chatter of New York, perhaps

some animate distortion caused by
silver-haired, or red, or long-eared bats
– who knows *exactly* when they stopped to comprehend
that most of what we thought we knew for sure

was now in doubt, the universe
more mystery than anyone imagined?
No limit to the possibilities;
or none we could detect?

I never had much time for schoolbook gods,
but *something* is in the details, *Ansatz, Geist,*
the shadow that drifts through the sensors, corrupting our data
for hours, until we notice that it's gone.

Octaves below the frequencies we hear
the background is a kind of music, harmonies
inferred from microwaves and static, heat
as shadow, or some flicker in the light

that could be you, or me, or someone else,
the man I might have been, the child he was,
blue in the folds of your heart,
where my blood is sealed.

STILL LIFE

You know where this work begins: a brace of quail
or woodcock; half a dozen

oysters, shucked, and spending in a slur
of milt and light; a bowl from Jingdezhen,

brought in, they say, as ballast for the tea,
(that blue and white the Chinese did not favour,

preferring single tones, say *lang yao hong,*
or *qingbai*, threads

of craquelure or pooling in the glaze
instead of narrative), the emblematic

lotus bloom or Willow Pattern scene
half-hidden by a heap of blemished grapes

and vineleaf, peaches, lemons with their rinds
half-peeled. It has nothing to do

with shellfish, nothing to do
with cherries, or the trade in porcelain,

but speaks of how the worm
is present, always: moments as they happen

perishable, married love and selfhood
perishable by their very

nature; yet, by nature, given back
in season, sieved

through clay and rain and fruit-falls for the meagre
gold of summer's end, the kitchen

silent, when you bring the apples in
and wrap them, individually, in sheets

of newsprint, humming torch songs as you work
till dusk, beyond the point where I am gone.

HENDRICK AVERCAMP: A STANDING MAN WATCHING A SKATING BOY

No doubt, in a year or two, this child will be gone;
rumours of war in the air and boys at that age
always impatient for something.
The wide road that leads to the pond runs all the way out
to the press gang – you can almost taste
the glare of blood, the panic in the ranks,
the dead laid out in seams of fire or lye
(*thus have they loved to wander;*
they have not refrained their feet);

but for now, he is safe; and the father admits
to a moment of guarded pride, which is never quite free
of misgiving (look at how close he stands
to where the boy is balanced on his skates, a kind
of beauty in the act of concentration).
We all have days like this, the quiet mind
dispensing with care to the greater or lesser extent
that circumstance allows: the steady light

above the frozen pond, the far-off
cries of other skaters, gangs
of schoolboys playing *kolf* amidst the crowds,
sleigh-bells, horse-bells, tradesmen, flocks of crows
come down to carrion: it has to be
a pleasure to be locked inside this maze
of noise and flow, of glint and spark and shadow.

This man won't go to war; he's too attuned
to maintenance and sleep, to being here
and knowing not to look
for trouble, since it's bound to look for him.

For those without power, this is what passes
for wisdom: a homespun mechanics

of knowing how much of the world is already decided,
the favoured trinket crushed beyond repair,
the last good apples blackening the grass
for days, before they blur into the rain,
the splay-crack in the ice, the hidden culvert,

how anything can burrow to the heart
or chill the soul: a black wind off the sea,
a confidence misplaced, some casual lie,
those days out when the party stays too long

and lets the fever in; and yet, till then,
he has those blessings he and his
can muster, bread and lard, a little jam,

some twigs of ivy in an old, chipped jug
his mother used to have; his boy; his wife;

such gladness as happens, kindling his mind like the sun.

STILL LIFE WITH FEEDING SNAKE

As soon as we consider a phenomenon in itself and in relation to others, neither desiring nor disliking it, we will in quiet attentiveness be able to form a clear concept of it, its parts, and its relations. The more we expand our considerations and the more we relate phenomena to one another, the more we exercise the gift of observation that lies within us. If we know how to relate this knowledge to ourselves in our actions, we earn the right to be called intelligent.

Johann Wolfgang von Goethe

That day, he covered the table
in plain white cloth;
then, carefully (the basic things
are hardest to perfect),
he set out a pair of hand-made
fruit bowls he had purchased on a whim,
shallow and powder blue,
like those mosses that grow
on barren slopes
high in the north, the glaze on them
uneven, heavy,
thicker at the rim,
the surface craze
still haunted by the kiln.

He had come to the point
of knowing he had to abandon
the best part of what he'd learned
from years of craft:
the blet of rot,
the snake-light in a vase

of tulips, all of memory and loss
suspended in the depths
of a reflection
Now, what he wanted
was texture: how it reconciles the mind
with gravity,
and gravity itself, made visible
in blues and greys, the one
inevitable fact,
other than light.

Mid-morning:
sun in the open
doorway, the weather
sedative,
he went to work.
The way to be slow,
so he thought,
was never to come to a stop
and so he was far away
from the given world,
when she came in out of the yard
and told him that, somewhere below,
in the crawl space
under his feet,
some kind of snake
was swallowing
some kind of bird.
– It's odd, she said
– it seems so very cruel,
and yet, it's somehow
chastening as well,
or if that's not the word,
then something like it.
She touched his arm
and looked him in the eye.

– Why don't you come
and see it for yourself?
Just come and take a look,
I'll show you where.

He was one of those men who feel shamed
when they find something ugly.
His lifelong discipline, he thought,
to remain impartial,
to consider each thing
in its own light, in quiet
attentiveness, neither
desiring nor disliking;
and yet he had always felt guilty
looking at animals,
even at the zoo, when he was
young, the seals
distracted from themselves by being
watched so much, the elephants
so alien
he never saw them clear.
That was the problem,
he thought: no living thing
could ever be seen enough;
and though he stared
and stared at it, the jaguar only seemed
a kind of sleep-made-flesh; the lemurs
gazed, for seconds, back into his eyes,
then turned away,
annoyed at having thought of him
as real.
So, that afternoon, engaged
with something else,
he had no wish to break off from his work
and follow her out to the yard;
and yet, because she needed him to see,

for reasons that went beyond
the bonds of marriage,
he knelt down by the steps and gazed
into the crawl space.
Immediately, he saw the gaping jaw,
the sure light of the predatory eye,
the snake itself
so close, and scarcely
darker than the dust in which
it lay, the bird
half-gorged, in spasm, not quite
dead, perhaps, but not quite
living, either.
He slowly found his feet. What could he say?
There was nothing to do here,
nothing to rescue, or kill.
They stood a moment, silent, not together;
and then, without speaking,
she walked into the house,
and he went back
to gravity and light.

That soul is incomplete, the heart
forever pilgrim,
this he did not doubt.
That blood is native
to the coldest rain, a dark
immensity of bruise and appetite,
he'd always understood;
but that afternoon,
with the image of what he had seen
gnawing at the far edge
of his mind,
he felt how disengaged he had become
from any world
that she could figure in.

He loved her still, but what he most loved now
was being there, alone, and glad of it,
at work, in play, awake to every choice
the body makes, unreasoning, and sure,
no matter what the heart
is meant to do:

and this was when he guessed − no great
epiphany, no Pentecostal fire,
but softly, as he felt the painting slide
away from him, no gravity, no light,
the Arctic blues, the emptiness he'd hoped
to find between the fruit bowls, where the shadow
thickened, all of it
distraction − *this*
was when he put his work aside
and went from room to room
seeking her out,
and finding her nowhere, not in their upstairs
study, not in the hall,
and not in the glossy
angle of the stairs
where, sometimes, on a summer's afternoon,
she sat with a tray of tea
and a favourite book.
It took him far too long to work it out,
but when he did, he ran into the yard
and found her, watching,
in a garden chair,
not morbid in the least, not even
curious, but thinking of the bird,
or so it seemed,
lending it what it could not
know or sense, but
willing, as its presence leached away,
some recognition of its suffering

and all the forms that suffering can take
in such a world, where everything must feed
and anything can be
demoted, in the merest
instant, to the role
of fodder, strayed, or careless
in its path,
and falling through the play of light and shade
to some dry pit, beneath the world it loves,
where something darker
than the usual dust
makes good on every tender thing it finds.

ANECDOTAL ACCOUNTS OF THE LAST
NORTHERN DYNASTY

No one has said
they're the last. Doves
come to the garden at daybreak; the fishpond
brightens as usual.
Women are planting rice
in the first spring warmth; an eel-trap
fattens in the dark gut of the river.
In rooms meant for other matters, people make love
through the long afternoons, while their spouses are somewhere else,
blissfully unaware, or blessed with the thought
that some far thing is larger than them all;
enough, now, to be present for the play
of light and motion: cart-ruts in the streets,
the market stalls
of fresh greens and persimmons.
Out by the kilns, a bargeman
pauses to watch
as a cormorant rises mid-stream;
he lingers a moment, and then he returns to his work,
loading his boat with the ash-pink or tangerine bricks
that some historian will later classify
as *typical*. No history, for now;
and no ambition;
only the weekday light on an empty yard
and the unexpected discipline
of being here
while nothing really happens.
No one has said they're the last and, besides,
it's not that an end is coming, or not
an end that could mean anything
to them:
the adulterers turning away to their different homes

with relief and regret,
the fisherman hauling his trap
from hairweed and mud,
and the painter who wakes every day, from an old man's sleep,
in the pine-scent and frost
of the village he knew as a boy,
to wander an hour or more in that upland light
before he remembers he left it years ago
for reasons he cannot recall.
Now home is his main intent
when he sets to work,
his wife dead, his daughters
married, the life of the town
an echo of itself, all fade and blur,
where nothing is sure
but the promise of rain by nightfall.
He wishes his mind could become
a meadow grazed by animals so wild,
he wouldn't even think
of naming them,
but day after day, that old light in his head
glimmers, then fades, as the fresh ink
dries on the paper.
Crocuses bolt through snow, a new foal
spills into a blear of warmth and straw,
but all the birds he ever knew by name,
lapwings and finches, pintails, the several larks,
are flitting away to the light of a different world,
a light from the south,
whose masters have yet to be born.

ANDREW WYETH: *EVENING AT KUERNERS*, 1970

If the soundtrack of their life is anything
to go by

the people downstairs are clearly
soft in the head,

a music you only hear elsewhere
in ringtones and jingles rising

nightly through the floor, not loud enough
to merit a complaint, but always

there, subliminal
and constant, like those cures you read about

in magazines, the pleasant,
airbrushed voice

recalling, again and again,
what you need to forget,

some sexual deviancy, perhaps,
or madness of the type

that, while not quite a threat, your loved ones find
embarrassing.

Lately, I find it difficult to sleep
but when I do I dream of a hotel

I stayed at once, the silence of its halls
a minor paradise

I didn't want to leave, a view
of tulip poplars looming up

at every window, gold
with autumn, as I walked the three flights down

to breakfast.
That was in Delaware, I think,

close to where an artist I admired
had painted winter scenes and country barns

and windows
with a clean wind blowing in.

Timing is always
a problem, but if I could

I'd die in such a place:
an old man taking the stairs

on principle, his head
a gallery of pictures he has seen

and nothing besides, save the sound of a country
river, its name

so musical it made him want to smile
before he stopped, to lean against the wall

for just a second, stopped
and almost caught his breath before

it snagged on something else
and bled away.

STILL LIFE WITH LOST COSMONAUT

If I imagine you dead, there is no love
immense enough to bring you back to earth;

but here, in this bowl of apples, on this kitchen
table, gold

and crimson in a space
that could not be more ample or precise,

I see you drifting in the selfsame light
that I inhabit, wishing not

to occupy, or slip loose, or possess,
life being more to me than I could ever

wish for, colour, shape, the subtleties
of shade and, when I bite into the fruit,

the taste of it, much more than I could
wish for; though I wish you could be here.

FATWA ON INTIMACY

There is no other love like surrogate.
Vertigo after you left, in the ruined

hive of what I used to think
was Thou.

Which I foresaw
and yet I waited years

through snow, then snowdrops,
crocuses, then sweet

viburnum.
Now, I assume,

you are working all night
at the lab,

the one light burning in that third-floor
window, clouds

of noctuids at the glass, while you extract
the venom, or the stunted embryo,

from something still alive, but scarcely
conscious in the cradle of your hand,

the weight of it, the pulse,
the veins of heat

a pleasure that must go without a name
for now, at least, the lacing in a wing

extended to its fullest and held still
for minutes, while you make the next incision.

GEORGE AND THE DRAGON

This killing will never stop.
It's not enough
to slay the beast, he has to make it clear
how calm his loathing is, how utterly devoid
of fellow feeling;
and though she is present,
the woman is incidental;
whatever he hoped in the past, he's not here, now,
for the wet of her mouth on his skin, or his curdled hands
tangling in the spilt folds
of her gown.
It isn't love he lacks. It's narrative.
The gown is red, which symbolises
otherworldly grace, or else
protection from some fever yet unnamed
– it's hard to say
what ritual this is. All we can know
for sure is that too much is being
sacrificed, the dragon with its throat
transpierced, a sign
left over from the damp, pre-Christian world,
led from the cave on its chain (the woman holds it
lightly in her hand) to be destroyed
for no good reason, given that it's tame
and captive now.
Perhaps it's just too green
or too expressive, set against this knight
whose mind is elsewhere, blank as ordinance
and formal, like the host, or like
this seeming bride-to-be, whose only love
is senseless *agape*.
No guessing what lightens their days; no guessing
how quietly each soul upholds its grey

dominion, at the near edge of a marsh
that runs into the dark
forever, gulls
and egrets flickering across
its waterlands, a salt wind in the grass
so like a voice, the body longs
to follow; though they never leave this spot
where flesh is conquered, time and time again,
the lance fixed in the dragon's
larynx, old blood
cooling in the sand, like candlewax,
the cave, a myth, the storm, mere ornament,
the new god in the throne room of high heaven,
observing our trespasses, judging us, keeping us pure.

FIRST EXERCISE IN ABANDONMENT

Some mate for life, like swans, and fold
immediately to bedrock monochrome

– and this I find
appealing, though it's never what I thought to want

for us. For us, the only narrative
is crimson, though we try to put it off

till later, drafting in such histories
of snow and widowhood that chance provides;

and what if you could see me well enough
to find that place where all I ever am

is Floating World,
now that a light is burning in the house

your father would not build
from old confetti?

No light we cannot dim, save memory,
no snowfall at the far edge of the mind

that cannot be espoused, a local
Edo, swift and imperceptible,

as wings are, when they flicker at the skin
then hurry on, beneath a darkening sky.

ANNUNCIATION IN GREY AND BLACK

Night at the edge of the world, where nothing
sings, except this mop-girl in her stonewashed
coveralls, the silted airport gloom
filming her hands like some ersatz account of sainthood.

A psalm from her mother's book, or a slum-town
dance tune disappears into the pleats
of fabric, when she bends into her work,
unnoticed, which is all she wants to be,

the last wave of passengers headed for Perth or Jakarta
already embarked, the beatitude of her skin
unnoticed, so she thinks she is

alone, her lips still moving when she turns
and sees me, sees me right down to the bone
of hurt and lust, a thousand miles from home.

APPROACHING SIXTY

Now that my ladder's gone,
I must lie down where all the ladders start
In the foul rag and bone shop of the heart.

W. B. Yeats

In the Central Café
in Innsbruck,
a girl in a dark-blue dress
unlooses her hair from its clasp
so it falls to her waist,
then sits with her friends
to coffee and *Sachertorte*,
turning her head just once
to look at me,
and all the while winding her hair
in knots and raising it high
so the nape of her neck
is visible, slender and pale
for moments, before the spill
of light and russet
falls down to her waist: falls
back down to her waist across the dark-blue
fabric, while I try hard not to stare:
a man growing old, with a touch
of sciatica, mild
arthritis
and hypertension,
striving to seem a comfortable kind
of scarecrow, not so blinded by desire
as makes the heart a nest of rag and bone,
and still, if she could see it,

not quite foul,
just one of those
who knows what beauty is
and lingers on the ache,
to stay alive.

HANDFASTING

Giraldus Cambrensis, an early Welsh chronicler, reported that in ancient Wales, parents would 'let' their daughter to a prospective husband, who would put down a sum of money. If the couple decided to part and not be married, he would have to pay a further fee to the parents.

George Monger: *Marriage Customs of the World*

Had he mastered the thin domain
of self-denial,
replacing the skin with sleep, an implacable snow
of mothering and cold valerian,
the house of Spoken Word and Christmas Morn
become the castle in a fairy tale
where hearts are hung to dry
on fatted string,
he might have guessed
the limits of their bargain.

The day he brought her home,
the land felt small
for miles around, cold fields of mud and rain;
and that first night,
his beasts called in the dark,
a run of panic
streaming through the yard,
cold in his feet and cold at the roots of his eyes
while he fumbled against her, fingerless
and dumb.

Days turned to weeks;
the weeks to months, then years;

he set aside his mother's favourite things
and bought the new one gifts, to exorcise
the ghosts she carried in
from who knew where;
till, finally, the house no longer his,
he gave it up and learned to love
its echo, rooms
of spice and bitumen,

his father's shadow standing in the hall
at first light, things to do, the cattle
gathered in the barn on market days;
and all the time, a sense of something
creaturely, behind the bedroom door,
more animal than human, so it made him
wonder what it was
he could have wanted,
or what he might have kept, had he but chosen
otherwise, what lost realm of desires

foregone, a body slipping from his grasp,
the way a guddled trout might shiver free
just at the very last: that lovely
emptiness it leaves
between the hands,
a puzzle of warmth
and marrow swimming away
to everywhere,
a stream inside the stream
of light and water, single, almost free.

A DEAD HARE, IN THE DRIVEWAY AT OVER KELLIE, 15TH OCTOBER 2015

I got home late that night, so I didn't see
the body, till the headlamps picked it out,
almost unscathed, so it seemed,
in the hover of light, the taxi-driver
stepping out to look, as I stooped down
and ran my fingers through the empty pelt.

No marks that I could see, no wounds
to tell how it had died, the driver
stepping out to look, unless he'd thought
to see me to the door,
sensing the blur in my hands, the house key
spilling from my fingers in the dark, the smell
of vodka on my breath.

By morning, the fur had creased
and shriveled, and the outcurve of the eye
was nothing but a smudge
of glaze and pulp, the limbs
extended, still, as if they could recall
the joy of bounding through the summer grass,
still formal, while its substance leached away
and left behind a corpse, abridged, unspooled,
all tenderness surrendered to the rain

so quietly, it made me want to stop
and let the spell come over me, a brief
rehearsal of the self shrugged off or pared
away, another body shining through
as skin and bone, perhaps, but with its light
intact, the tawny camber of the soul
protracted, till the chance of something new
seemed possible, if only for an hour.

AN ESSAY IN *SANGFROID*

> *Go to, I'll no more on't; it hath*
> *made me mad. I say, we will have no more marriages:*

Shakespeare

Narrowest of loopholes, love
is not the martyry we took it for
in sleepless adolescence, cobalt blue

as portage, windows
feathered through the night
with tufts of frost.

Had we but known that we so loved the cold
as children
there would be no marriages,

only the little death of going out
at dewfall, shivers
wickering the skin,

a clearing in the woods where, now and then,
we pause for witcheries we only half
imagine, faces

grinning from the dark,
a boyhood walking home, in autumn rain,
chill with the hope of being left unmastered.

MISTAKEN FOR A UNICORN

Give me the better reason to desist
that no one else has heard

so clearly as the wet edge of a blade
slipping through graven flesh.

We've come too far to call this beautiful,
(though beauty is its best

approximation)
and nothing intercedes

for pleasure, since we let the dragon fade
to spots of tapestry and cochineal.

No flicker of the tongue that would have greened
the wildwood of the heart with sap and flame,

though green was the catastrophe
we prayed for, when we thought this life was real

as wounding is, the tempering of nerve
and tendon by the touch it least desires

and aches for, like that sound a forest makes
when darkness falls and every bird is still.

SWEETNESS

*What good is the warmth of summer, without the cold of winter
to give it sweetness?*

John Steinbeck

Who was it brought the tallow for this lamp
you light against the darkness, while my dogs
go hungry?

No barter is permitted in this place.
No credit given.

You've slept through long extinctions, new
advances in the management of pain,

but this is not a dream you get to dream
in crinolines.

This morning, someone found an animal.
It must have dragged itself across the snow
for miles, until the first dog caught its scent.

The rest were quick to follow.

Perhaps it was this flame
that lured it in,

wounded and starved, it may have hoped
to find us merciful.

I don't know what it was. There's only bone
and rosaries of gore
unstitching in the snow.

I wish we could have seen:
we might have named it;

though nothing could be done against the dogs.
We'll need them soon. Supplies are running low.

THE LAZARUS TAXA

Still they stood,
A great wave from it going over them,
As if the earth in one unlooked-for favour
Had made them certain earth returned their love.

Robert Frost

If anything is safe
to love, it is

the jellyfish, *Aurelia aurita*,
that pink and silver

moon–cloud, drifting wild
in every harbour from the South

Atlantic
to the Bay of Reykjavik;

or *Hippocampus*,
monstrous to the Greeks,

though shaped like horses,
gentle as the wind

in August:
moving softly through

the weeds, the brood male
gathers the eggs in his pouch

like treasure, while the female swims away
to miles of seagrass; coral;

predators.
                    If anything is safe
to love, it has to be

the Starry Smooth-Hound,
gliding through the bright

salt water, innocent
of need, its joys

too quick to be remembered
or betrayed.

I would not choose the Bluefin
Tuna, Hector's

Dolphin, or the Humphead
Wrasse.
                    Right Whale, Blue Whale, Fin

Whale, Yangtze Finless
Porpoise, and the Maltese Ray

are equally unpromising,
(they will not be here long).
                                        In years to come,

the market will experience
a glut in holy relics, scraps of bone

and slivers of dubious tissue, hermetically sealed
in ampoules, with old diagrams

of how things would have looked
had they survived,

convenient gifts
for those who would believe

that absence is its own
reward, a cybernetic

fiefdom of Saxon
gold, the cold

dead-end
as hallows.

If any man were safe
to love, it would be

Lazarus, awake between two worlds,
until a word recalls him from the field

where he had strayed, bereft of song and flight
(no live birds in that place, no

parakeets or hooded orioles;
only the script of Archaeopteryx

consigned, but not reduced
to blueprint

in the marled folds
of hereafter).

The moment he turns,
he finds the world transformed,

the animals he knew, the ox, the ass,
the cattle in the fields, the flocks

of vultures over bloody Golgotha,
all gone, and in their place

a host of resurrections, long-lost
fishes, given up

for dead,
amphibians

and mammals, skipper flies
and pine voles come to life

forever, as he blindly makes his way
through gardens of round-leafed birch

and café marron, the fountains
teeming with Black Kokanee,

painted frogs,
Latimeria

chalumnae, Latimeria
menadoensis

and, out in the furthest shade
of the jellyfish trees,

Mahogany Gliders,
calling his name in the dark,

as if, for now,
the earth returned his love.

JEAN SIMÉON CHARDIN: *PERDRIX
ROUGE MORTE, POIRE ET COLLET
SUR UNE TABLE DE PIERRE*, 1748

Dead, it has become a different species,
exempt from a plot in which tenderness plays no part,
exempt from wind and ice, but not this light
that lingers in the plumage like the hand
that teased it from the noose and laid it out
to show the varying colours.
Autumn is in the woods, a gradual chill
that creeps across the orchard day by day:
dewfall on the grass, then morning frost,
the body that snags in the tines, when I rake the leaves,
a mystery, part-flesh, part-interregnum.
I will not call it *vole*. It's something else,
just as the bird is, dead, in the oil and pigment,
and what it is that lingers past the point
where anything is absent, what it is
that slips away, I do not wish to name.
Ansatz. Geist. The shadow in the woods
that isn't what I know it ought to be,
the shadow in the tide, trailing the boat
for hours, until we notice that it's gone –
and this is all we have
to work with, something far-fetched in the heart's
geography, a thin path running out
to empty shoreline, miles of reed and sky.
Full moon, out on the coast road.
An unsolved grief returns to scatter
windrows in the skin, like lines of ink
in running water, always not quite there,
but never gone.
If only our priests and teachers
had told us, back in Sunday Bible Class,

that all the afterlife this life could promise
was stitched into some moister
incurve of the body, white
and precious, like a silkworm in the dark,
if only they had told us, years ago,
how everything seems less material
as time runs on,
the partridge on its back, the empty snare,
the stitched black of the eye, the way the feathers
thin, or how a body, when it dies,
relaxes by degrees into the cold
and is not born again, but hurries on
to other bodies, flecked with paradise.

PLUVIOSE

There is a kind of sleep that falls
for days on end, the foothills lost in cloud,
rain in the stairwells, rainspots crossing the floor
of the Catholic church

and the sense of a former life
at the back of our minds,
as if the dead had gathered here in shapes
that seemed at least familiar, if not perfect.

As children, we were told they came
for our sakes, bringing secrets from the cold,
the loam on their eyes and hands
a kind of blessing,

but now they are here,
in the creases and lines on our skin,
speaking through us to friends we have never seen,
or only to the rain, because it sounds

the way it sounded once, when they were young,
setting a ladle aside, or a finished book,
and the world almost come to an end,
when they stopped to listen.

Late afternoon, and further along the canal
the lock-keeper's prettiest daughter is setting
eel traps in the clockless silt and purl
of waters her mother fished, before marriage and barter,

and though she has been dead for forty years,
she is living the life I lost on the way to school

in the body I failed to grow up in, her hands in the flow
of the river, finding the current

and teasing it loose, like a story, the word by word
of trains running through in the dark, in the seasonless rain,
and the faces in every compartment familiar and strange,
with a sister's disdain, or a grandmother's folded smile.

CRANE-WATCHING IN OSTPRIGNITZ-RUPPIN, NOVEMBER 2014

for Lucas

There is too much light in the world
to bear the weight
of Euclid, too much
fog, with shore birds, bright in the salt-water channels
thinning the sands, the Black-Tailed

Godwit, the Curlew
Sandpiper, named
from the field guide, but still
uncertain, still
defiantly heraldic.

I've lived through days like these
before and scarcely
noticed, skylarks
hidden in my sleeves, whole afternoons
of stork

and oriole.
I've learned to recognise
their several customs,
how some birds appear on the wind, while others
arrive in a flurry of snow

from who knows where,
finding the last of the haws
on a thorn tree, then gusting away

in a scatter of shadow
and ice,

and these are the ones I have loved, beyond all
geometry: snow bunting, fieldfare,
waxwing – it barely
matters, when the whole idea
is colour:

how, sleepless and given to bouts
of fasting, I have come to share their hoard
of pearl-grey and blue
and scarlet, as I vanished from a world
I've had to learn by rote

since I was born.
Maybe it's what I guessed at, years ago,
coming from church to something not yet
visible, but felt,
along the hedge, a weather

quietly set aside, while I laid
the table, all the while
conscious that something was there, at the scullery door,
or pressed to the kitchen window, the green of it
urgent as rain.

To think that so little persists
beyond that unlearning:
another gravity,
a subtler motion;
but, given the choice,

I would live at the end of the season,
forever:

the last day of autumn,
the men at the Linum fish-house
laughing and cracking jokes

as the dark seeps in,
night on the ponds,
where the next wave of cranes have come
to gather in their thousands,
gorgeous

ciphers of grey and crimson
vanishing into the reeds
as they settle down.
On Hauptstrasse, under the streetlamps,
the stalls are piled with gourds

and pumpkins, brick red and butter
yellow, finely
ridged or smooth as glass.
An owl calls from the far end of the track
that runs out to a wash of marsh and sky,

then everything is still: the street, the moon,
the fish-house, with its red and yellow
lanterns draped on lines along the pier,
making a place like home, from a little light,
their muddled reflections spotted with pondweed and stars.

CONFITEOR

I heard something out by the gate
and went to look.
Dead of night; new snow, the larch woods
filling slowly, stars beneath the stars.
A single cry it was, or so it seemed,
though nothing I had recognised as native;
and when it came again, I knew for sure.
No badger there. No gathering of deer.

Forgive me, if I choose not to believe
the snow would fall like this, were I not here
to see it.
There might be snow, of course, but not like this,
no hush between the fence line and the trees,
no sense of something other close at hand,
my dwindling torch-beam flickering between
a passing indigo and *lux aeterna*.

I stood a while to listen;
nothing moved
– and then I turned and walked back to the house,
the porch light spilling gold for yards around,
snow at the open door and then, again,
that far cry in the dark behind my back
and deep in the well of my throat
as I live and breathe.

IN PRAISE OF FLIGHT

*Vous connaissez sans doute un voilier
nommé 'Désir'*

Henri Laborit

Like ruined churches in another snow
that lengthens everything to nightfall, even

faith itself, that simple dynamo
we never thought to lose,

the old machines are waiting in their skins
of lubricant and dust to run again,

a generation's span of *Caritas*
and train rides to the ocean with a favourite

uncle, summer rain and gabardine,
the blue of empty windows miles from home

a vast and beatific
absence, applebound

and starlit.
Though unconfirmed, our better selves report

that everything we need, from hereon in,
is present in the drag of pendulum:

the minutes running down, the warranties,
the half-lives amortised against

an overall momentum, animus
and instance, not confused so much as

venturing on play, as if
the stalled hope in the works was more in doubt

than waking in a budget-priced hotel,
the phone switched off, while thirteen floors below

our fêted doubles trail us, street to street,
like Arctic hunters, doused in alpenglow.

SPRING

Gerard Manley Hopkins

Winter is gone to ground, form sinks to black
in minuscule abandon:

mouse bones snagged on pea-sticks, wells of fern,
midden and matter, behemoth and mustardseed.

Locked behind ivy and glass, and faintly
animate,

the life everlasting
thickens to woodlouse and gore;

and every year, we pray a spring will come
to comprehend it, all this juice and joy

informing a world we would not dare to master.
Inhuman plenty: caribou and crane,

tectonic shifts of eel and buffalo,
pink-foot and greylag goose, vast shoals of herring,

salmon in their millions, pouring live
through fractured dams at Alta and Spokane

– *strain of the earth's sweet being*, Ghost Dance and Dreaming:
awake for its own sake, *in saecula saeculorum*.

DOMESTIC BLISS

This I remember:
something on a blade
that nobody could name,
and all the colours
bleeding into one
slow red;
the smell of sugar
on my mother's clothes
the day she fell
and broke her collarbone;
the baby falling silent
in her blood,
the weight of it inside her
like a bell.

When love is gone
there is no substitute
for iodine;
wounds I had kept for years
in the folds of a shirt
brought to fruition, now,
in the memorised world
we spelled out
from the Book of Genesis.
Why it should be so sparse
I never asked,
a bucket filled
with razor shells
and whelks

and something alive
inside, the salt
and suction of it

blue as paraffin,
but gone to vapour
every time I tried
to name it; gone,
the way a cut was gone
and left no scar, but
lingered, like a touch,
a steadfast warmth
I would not choose again,
and scarcely feel
although I long for ruin.

SOME ANECDOTAL NOTES ON
SLEEP DISORDERS

In the small hours, there is nothing to believe
and no emotion, other than the heart's
Victoriana (picture books and militaria

beguiling us from pit towns, where we lie
in icy beds, a parliament of owls
conjured from the distance in the trees

and no beyond,
the Mains House, with its rattan silences,
a layman's guide to broderie

and pain-as-discipline, the rod
no thicker than the knuckle
of a thumb).

Expert in this for years, mediciner
of like cures like, tisanes and simples
archived in a thousand languages,

I find no secret passage in the dark
to where the others dream, through fern and rain,
my mother, in her jade and amber dress,

drifting to sleep in the radio's smoke and mirrors,
satsumas in a bowl and, through her breathing,
Nilsson and Björling, live, from the back of beyond.

Frost today; a scuffed white on the roads
from street to street, where nobody will wake
for years, the Cousteau-blue
of TV at each window like the room
where Beauty sleeps, with all her beasts intact.

No one could rouse her now; that day has passed:
no orchard at the far end of the lane,
no yew walk through the churchyard, just a cold
hardstanding where a stick of lodgepole pine
stands decked with wires and pallid Xmas lights,

as if the festival were here, and not
a cry beyond our limits, when the night
steals in, and something overtakes the land
so utterly, you'd think it was a god.

TO THE SNOW QUEEN

Quest'è l'verno, ma tal che gioia apporte

Antonio Vivaldi

If you think she exists like that, you should think again.
It's winter now, and love is not the question.

Children see wolves through the trees
and the beauty astounds them.
Winter, they say; *it's winter, and joy is the question.*

Mistake her for what you will: when she stands in your path
at evening, she is not
the enemy you always hoped to find.

Her boarhounds await her command; they are always
more than predators
and joy is what they live for, heedless joy.

Whatever we bring to the forest is not enough.
No safety precautions; no field guides; no grandfather's compass.

Children walk home from school in twos and threes
with mandarins and cloves and lengths of ribbon.
Some call her name in the dark.
                              She will never choose *them*.

POEM ON A LINE OF GEORGE SEFERIS

The houses I had they took away from me.

George Seferis
tr. E. Keeley and P. Sherrard

I   ILLEGALS

The little I know of houses
I learned from the rain.
The houses I had,
they took away from me:
gilt frames and slipware
buried in the hedgelines,
bedsheets and tatting
tossed into the fire,

till nothing remained but a faint
nostalgia for the laws of maintenance,
moss hair and eggshells
scraped from the rim of a downpipe,
artesian wells
of tangleweed and feathers,
the toxins of an unrequited boyhood,
relics in jam-jars, blueprints in crayon and blood.

On autumn nights
I walk from street to street
in search of something I would surely know
if only I could find it: beds
of winter heliotrope; Parthenocissus
clinging to the walls around

78

an unlit casement
where I would have slept

alone, my Oxford Children's
Classics stacked
around me, like that
forest where the huntsman reconsiders,
sheathes his icy blade
and walks away,
leaving the child to nightfall
and the wolf.

Twenty years later, the son of a seventh son
wakes in a shroud of lice
and wants for something true, like love, or distance,
a thousand miles of darkness at his back,
railway stations, signals, cattle trains,
the men in uniform who burned
the bodies: boys
and women; common-law

uncles; beasts
of burden – it was all the same
abandonment, sheer
weight and that annulment in the light
that makes us think of everything
as Mother.

★

Wagtails in the snow
under a fig tree;
unripe fruits, like tumours
rimmed with ice.

The houses I had, they took away from me:
at times, with my consent; at times quite –

imperceptibly, as anyone might cross
a backlot of *palo verde* in the first

shimmer of creosote, blankness in the eyes
as they moved off in single

file, a few of them
women, but mostly

boys in ragged shirts
and stained *huaraches*,

skirting the walls and glimmering away
from that motel in Ajo where we stopped

to pass the night (looking for birds
in Southern Arizona):

a pallor to one boy's face, like the faded
chollas in the yard, and that same

promise, through it all,
of reinstatement.

Illegals, you said, when I told you,
though what I saw

reminded me more
of my grandmother, three weeks away

from Dublin,
heading blindly to Crosshill,

a girl with a cardboard suitcase
and broken shoes

her coat too thin
against the coal-town frost –

⋏

The first group left at dawn
with nothing but what they could carry,
crossing the bridge
where rock creepers threaded the air
with a perfect attention,
then climbing the first steep meadow, cicadas
streaming away at their feet, the blet
of soakaway blacking the path, as they passed
through sheep folds, a flock of bells
retreating into the blue
of rock slip and pine,
the meadow giving way
to alpine flora – gentian, saxifrage,
improbable buttons of perfume
cradled in stone.

There is the temptation, always,
to be happy:
sufficient for the day,
all passion spent,
the first light singling out
those details where the eye could learn to see,
if not a god, then something
orderly: a shiver in the grass;
a wind moving over the waters –

but nothing you see here is true, save the wind
and the lives of others.
The lives of others, waiting to be witnessed.
The soul as shadow, waiting to be fleshed.

★

How gladly I would have fleshed the silhouette
that came at nightfall to my mother's
roseraie, its eager, blunted head
snuffling through thorn and bonemeal in the dark,

I cannot tell.
It might have been the wolf, come back
to call me out,
it might have been the mother of my dreams

made animate, a shape I would have seen
on *Zoo Time*, quasi-active for the sway
of torchlight in a theatre of rain.
There might have been a voice. Not just the thin

glissando in a stand of trillium, and not
the shimmer of snow on a twig, where a passing redpoll
paused in its flight
to listen: Brother? Stranger? Who could tell?

Imagine it is snowing in the first
fairy tale you ever got to hear
in this life. Refugees
are flooding across the border,

a sound you should have known from long ago:
the last of the year's
cicadas, prayer wheels
clicking in the wind.

Someone has left a garment of swansdown and sand
at the end of your bed:
ice on the collar, bloodstains on the cuffs,
that smell of acetone or cordite from the day

the huntsman left, his name erased
forever.
No appellations now: not even *exile*.
All you can do is walk, till the sun goes down.

All you can do is find what will suffice.

★

I'm not speaking to you about things past,
I'm speaking about love.

My Lares and Penates, substitutes:
knuckles of glass
and shards of lusterware,
dubious coins
and pipe stems packed with clay.

I know very little of houses, and yet I have guessed
that those who know nothing at all are those who build
to keep the stranger out, the wolf at bay,
the serpent crushed
beneath a virgin's heel.

Now all that remains is to open the kitchen door
and leave it open.
Nothing to see:
no talking animals;
no ravens in a pool of carrion.

The wolf is gone, though sometimes we believe
another shape will slip into the house,
tracking us down for one last fairy tale
where love is still a name
for transformation;

and everything you know
of Everafter
alters when you smell
the breath of it, the language
darkened in its mouth, the words

for *dead*
and *living*, sweet
and interchangeable, the heart
repealed by its disdain
for the beyond.

Whatever I know of houses
I learned from the creatures.
The houses we had, they took away from us,
sold, or demolished, the plaster broken down
to chalk marks in the rain, the doors and windows
shattered.

Everything lost. The firstborn. The wolf in its lair.
Nostalgia for the other animals
eaten away, like a snared limb, gnawed to the bone,
the marrow spilling, wet
and ash-pink in the snow.

But leave the door ajar
for what will come:

fires on the border at nightfall;
wolves at the treeline.

Some things are lost for weeks
before they are missed:

the cold viridian of spotted medick
caught in the steady bleed of an upland rill;

the last sheep drifting homeward from the hills,
its face a maze of wind and foreign joy.

Some things are lost forever. The word for *hawk*
or *blizzard* in a mountain dialect,

the method for making flatbreads, or damson brandy,
passed down from father to son, till the last son dies

in a volley of friendly fire
on the road to town.

He'd gone to cut agar; he'd walked out to gather honey;
he had nothing to do that day, and the air was sweet.

His killers had the wrong intelligence.

– But this is not the house we came to find:

a house full of voices and laughter, a house bright with rain,
            a large house with many windows . . .

If we speak about *broken*, or *lost*, the entire
history evades us:

beauty and *sadness*,
a smudged moon over the orchard,

the thrush in the garden
smashing a snail on a stone.

> *Sing little Antigone, sing, O sing . . .*
> *I'm not speaking to you about things past, I'm speaking*
> *about love.*

★

We waited days to see the snow that fell
this evening:

local at first, then
blinding, it blanks the windows,

fledges the blue
of the cypress, illumines each room

like the limelight in silent movies.
I go about the house, becoming strange

as I pull the blinds, the headlamps from passing cars
whiting me out, the clock in the hallway

suspended: *this*
is theatre, *this*

is live.
So much of it that cannot be

accounted for.

On an evening like this, in the winter of '62,
my grandmother closed her eyes,

the chain of a rosary
sliding away through her fingers,

as if she had just that moment understood
there was nowhere to go

but *out* through a gap
in the fabric of all she knew

to the one place where history ends.
Seven years old, I pictured it

as heaven: coal-town
roses, miles

of sunlight at the door
and everyone come back

to listen, fields
of concord

and attention, ancient
kinfolk on the threshold, suddenly

articulate.

★

but didn't we come this way
before?
climbing the narrow path
from a nameless harbour:
acres of heath
and birdcalls in the folds
of memory; our kinsmen
strangers on the road
with AKMs?

Once, I looked out on the land
as a promise of harvest:

> *Bright as shines the sun at noon,*
> *Or at night the silver moon,*
> *Sweet as fields with flowers and grass*

No harvest left.
No song from the neighbouring village.

The bones of our dancing
catalogued and bound,
the last of our love songs

boxed in the silk
clerestories of Paris
and New York.

We came this way before
through weeks of snow
forgetting all we knew; forgetting

Recipes for *kibbeh*, wedding songs,
bidos and flatbreads, all the words for snow,
springtime on the upper
meadow, when the gentians are in bloom,
the bird that came to meet us that first
morning, when we crossed the lower field
and started south.

> Then I said to my children, it's
> morning, the sun is up,
> bread on the table, butter, a bowl of eggs,
> a jar of phlox and jasmine by the window.

Every day, we walked down to the shore,
the house awake behind us, like a witness:
deep rooms lined with books, a winding stair,
years of sleep and snow-lit conversations,
sitting up late in the kitchen, the door standing open,
deer on the coast road, little owls scouting the walls

★

To believe in the right of all
to believe in nothing;

to feel an energy we cannot name
kindled around us;

to have and to hold
in season; to lay aside;

to climb a hill and come into the house
we hoped for
                    – a house by the sea –

light in the hall like a waiting
animal,

our lives a gift the land has always had
for idle dreaming

★

Driving north, the homesteads fallen now;
roof-beams and footings buried in moss and bracken, viscid
tissue in the gaps between the stones,
half-walls and hollows, spills of brick and glass;
and what was once a threshold or a stairwell
coloured now with willow-herb
and fuchsia
            (a tenancy, no more: our occupation
fleeting; ownership
a lie);

and home a random matter: transitory,
provisional;
somewhere you find by chance
on a warm afternoon:
a pond in the woods, amidst birch trees,
the last of the rain
misting the road to the village beyond the hill;

or the line you just crossed on the drive
to Wuppertal, or Paterson, New Jersey,
and suddenly the land is bright
with snow: the blur of it
falling all morning here, while you
were busy at home, preparing to close the house

for winter: the radio on
and that scent at the cellar door that makes you

wonder if someone is there, though you know for a fact
that you live by yourself
and that door has been locked for years.

The houses I had. The houses I cannot remember.
The meadow I mowed; the orchard, where, long ago,
we sat out late and talked beneath the stars,
bread on the table, wine glasses clouding with pollen.

Then I found myself in a mansion I did not know,
going from floor to floor, from room to room,
in search of a face, a shadow, a voice I remembered,
a mirror to guide me, a hallway, an unmade bed.

Nothing I saw was familiar, the windows kept changing,
and yet there was something so perfect about the light
that I barely had time to notice how far I had gone.
How far I had travelled from all I had lost or broken.

How, once and for all, the cicadas had ended their song.

ACKNOWLEDGEMENTS

Acknowledgments are due to the *London Review of Books*, in which several of these poems were first published. Also to the *New Statesman*, and to *Atlanta Review, Hampden-Sydney Poetry Review, Ploughshares, Sou'wester* (USA) and *Akzente* (Germany).

'Still Life' was commissioned for the Arden anthology *On Shakespeare's Sonnets: A Poets' Celebration,* edited by Hannah Crawforth and Elizabeth Scott-Baumann.

'Spring' was commissioned for *The Voice and the Echo* reading series at Shakespeare's Globe Theatre.

The title poem was inspired by a photograph sent to me from his home in Arizona by my friend Gerry Morgan. This poem is for him.

Still Life with Feeding Snake was published with the support of the Service de la Culture of the Canton du Valais, Switzerland, the Spycher: Literaturpreis Leuk and the Deutscher Akademischer Austauschdienst, (DAAD). My profound gratitude to all for their continuing support.